Apps

Beginner's Guide For App Programming, App Development, App Design

D0710845

Disclaimer Notice:

Please note the information contained within this document is for educational and entertainment purposes only. Every attempt has been made to provide accurate, up to date and reliable complete information. No warranties of any kind are expressed or implied. Readers acknowledge that the author is not engaging in the rendering of legal, financial, medical or professional advice.

By reading this document, the reader agrees that under no circumstances are we responsible for any losses, direct or indirect, which are incurred as a result of the use of information contained within this document, including, but not limited to, — errors, omissions, or inaccuracies.

Table of Contents

Introduction

Where do you get your best ideas? Did you wake up one morning and found that you had the perfect idea for the perfect app in your head? Something that has never been done and that you just know is going to take off like a shot?

The only thing is, although you have this fabulous idea, you have absolutely no idea how to turn it into a bestselling app. You don't know how to design, how to code, where to even begin. Don't despair because this book contains the 12 steps that you need to know to bring that idea out of your mind and onto smartphones and tablets everywhere.

App creation is not all that difficult, once you know which direction you are going in and as long as you can follow simple instructions. Let's make a start and get you on the right path to becoming a master app builder!

Chapter 1: The Different Types of Apps

We hear the word "app" used so much that we forget its origins. It used to be that an app was a word only used on big corporations, as recently as 5 years ago. So, how did it become such a popular term today and why has it become the most dominant word in technology?

Apps vs Software

So, what is the difference between the two? I'll tell you now, if you ask 200 people that question, I guarantee you will get 200 different answers! The word "software" is one that covers a whole host of different things, all the way from the latest Call of Duty up to Microsoft Office or Photoshop. Apps are partly software. In traditional terms, software is a product that is packaged whereas an app is a small piece of code that is for a specific use. Apps are built for everything – mainframes, servers, mobile or desktop computers and they may not always need an internet connection to work. The real difference lies in what you mean by the word "app".

When someone says "app" to you, no doubt you automatically think of a mobile app, ones that you download from iTunes or Google Play Store. These place an icon on your mobile device and you access the app through that icon. These can be somewhat challenging to create as each app has to be created separately for each different mobile platform. You couldn't build an app for iOS and expect it to work on Android, for example, because the code cannot be shared.

The Different Types

A mobile web application is accessed via the browse on the mobile device and need access to the internet to work. Websites such as Facebook and Twitter have both a mobile web application and a mobile application as well as a desktop application and many websites are designed around mobile use these days.

Web applications use a desktop web browser to work and many people get confused about the difference between a web application and a web site. It can be confusing but it's important to remember that an application is small and are designed to do something specific. Think about the photography sites such as Flickr; sites like LinkedIn or Yahoo Mail accessed on your tablet or phone. They are web applications whereas a page showing the marketing details for a company is most likely to be a website.

Desktop apps only run on desktop computers and do not require access to the internet to work. They may be accessed through icons on your desktop and many are standard additions on brand new computers. Examples of desktop apps include iPhoto, Paint and Notepad.

Consumer Changes

The way in which we use technology today has changed a lot. Traditionally, we needed IT systems and experts to help us find our way around, and find new applications and new software. Apps were mostly designed to be used for business tasks. These days, even your granny probably uses a smartphone to send pictures of her bridge game to a friend!

The modern app for mobiles are easier to use than the older packaged software's because they are driven by the fact that they are task specific. Mobile apps are easy to find, you simply visit the app store for the mobile platform you are using. You can find both web and mobile apps by using Google, Yahoo! Or another search engine and you will often find a write-up about the app, along with ratings and user reviews.

Installing an app is dead dimple, taking no more than a tap of the "Install" button. Many web apps and some mobile apps don't even need to be installed to be used. Finding the app you want for a specific task is easy; mobile apps are listed by category in the app stores and, when you find what you want, simply download it to take care of one purpose.

These days, the speed with which apps are developed and introduced to the market is amazingly fast. Many are released in a beta period first, allowing people to test them out, see if it's something they would buy. A high proportion of app developers are freelance these days and the field has grown by 8% in the last couple of years. And, the amount of apps being developed means that there are far more products on the market.

The very nature of a mobile app leads to quick launching and, because they are task specific, there is no need for a developer to create large tools or integrate complicated databases in the app, making them much simpler and easier.

Web apps may be designed for a specific browser, or a specific device and mobile apps support specific platforms. That means there is no need to add in extra planning to make the app work on a specific device, just the platform.

Wireless

Lastly, we know that the internet is an integral part of life; no longer do we go out and buy music or game CD's; we simply purchase them on the internet. We can watch movies, TV shows, videos, play games, get whatever information we need, and communicate with others.

Tablet and smartphone sales are rising fast, heading to take over from the desktop PC or the laptop. While these larger machines will always have a place in society, more and more people are using mobile, even large corporations.

Right now, the mobile app is the top of the heap, the most popular and the most used. They can be produced quickly, they are easy to use, can be used on the internet and fit whatever device they are being used on.

Now you know the difference between all the different types, let's start looking at what you need to get that app out of your head and into an app store near you.

Chapter 2: What Do You Need?

Now it's time to start thinking about getting that app out of your head and onto your computer. In order to be successful at creating an app, there are certain things you are going to need.

A Good Powerful Computer

You are going to need a high-end computer. Yes, you can use a mediocre one and there are development kits that you can use with a computer that isn't quite so powerful. But, having a high-end computer means that you will be able to test out your app far more efficiently. That way, you don't get disappointed users by giving them an app that is full of problems and bugs.

Having a good computer is highly recommended if you are intending to develop your app for the Android platform. Android emulators need heavy resources, including a very fast processed and a lot of spare RAM to run the Android emulators. If you use a computer that isn't quite up to spec, the Android emulators will run very slowly, if at all and you will spend your time fighting crashes and slow-downs.

A normal desktop PC is enough to build apps for both Windows and Android. If you are planning to develop a Windows app, you will need to make sure you are running the Windows 8 operating system. If, on the other hand, you are intending to build an app for the iOS platform, you will need a Mac as the development tools can only be found on the OS X operating system. As an absolute minimum, your Mac should be running on Snow Leopard but if you can get Mavericks or Yosemite, that's even better. A Mac Mini is sufficient although, if you want to beef things up, go for an iMac of the desktop. If you want one that is portable, look at the MacBook Pro and the MacBook Air.

You don't specifically need to have a large display to create a good app. However, they do give you a distinct advantage in that a lot of the development tools are faster and are more convenient on a larger screen. If you can afford it and are serious about becoming a developer, you could also go for a multi-screen setup but that is maybe something to think about later on down the line – let's see how your first app goes.

A Mobile Device

When you are developing a mobile app, you need to have a compatible mobile device to hand. There's a good chance you already have a tablet or a smartphone anyway so this is the easy bit. However, it is highly recommended that you use a separate device for development purposes, rather than using your everyday device. This can work out expensive, especially if you are preparing to develop and iOS app but it is a worthwhile investment. As you are just beginning though, and you may be on a tight budget, it's OK not to have the separate device. You must keep in mind though, that your device must match that of the market you are targeting – simply, if your app is for smartphones, you need to have one and if it is for tablets, well, you need to have one of those.

Choosing the device is the first part; there is still plenty more that you must take into consideration. First, your device must be of a good spec, i.e. good processor, RAM, reasonable battery life and a good screen size. Second, your device must be updated to the latest possible operating system for the platform you are on. It might seem like a god idea to develop an app that is compatible with earlier versions, so that you are targeting those that don't update their systems but you are also setting yourself some limitations that are not necessary.

Your mobile device is going to be a beta tester. You might wonder why you need this is the development tools already have emulators in them but the answer is simple. The emulator works on your computer and, to date, nobody has come up with a computer-based emulator that matches the way the mobile devices run. The emulators are useful for testing to see if there are any bugs in the app but the user-experience can only be tested on the device itself. You will be able to see how the app works with the touch screen and there are other things that you will only spot if you test on a mobile device.

The Right Software

Each separate platform has their own development tool kits. To create an app, you need to have the correct SDK – Software Developers Kit – for the platform you are working on. For iOS, you need the iOS SDK for the relevant iOS version that you are developing for. You would also need something called Xcode, which you can get from the Apple Developers website.

For Android, you will need the correct SDK and a program called Eclipse. The recommended SDK is 3.0 as it is compatible with the highest number of devices but, if you want to take advantage of the advanced features in the API, you should download the most up to date version.

For Windows apps, you will need to download Microsoft Visual Studio, which contains an integrated SDK; you can get this from the Windows Phone site.

Register as a Developer with Your Chosen Platform

To be able to download all these tools you first have to register. If you choose iOS, you will need to register with the official Apple Developers program.

This will cost you $99 a year ONLY if you want your app in the app store. Otherwise, registration is free.

Google is the same system except its only $25 per year and, for Windows, you need to go to the official Windows Phone site. Again, it is free to register but, when you are ready to publish, it will cost you $49 per year.

As soon as you have registered, all the development tools become open to you.

A Little Knowledge of Programming

You don't need to have degree in programming to become a developer. There are loads of web-based interfaces that can help you to create an app without having any knowledge of programming or coding; all you need to be able to do is click and drag.

However, I would recommend that you get some understanding of how to code and program as it opens up the way for more options. You don't need to go to college to do this; you can learn it all on the internet. Pick your language and find out as much as you can about the principles of it before you begin creating your app:

- SWIFT

- Objective C

- Objective C+

- JAVA

- XML

- CSS3

- HTML 5

- XAML

Once you are prepared, we can move on to looking at the 12 steps you need to go through in order to create, develop and design your mobile app.

Chapter 3: 12 Steps to Publishing Your Mobile App

The following 12 steps will give you an overview of the route you need to take, to go from thinking about your idea to actually publishing it. The development tools themselves contain all the help and information you need to build your app so I will not go into any details here.

Define Your Goal

That idea you woke up with this morning is your starting point. However, before you get into the nitty gritty of actually doing something with it, you need to be able to define the mission your mobile app has, what its purpose is. What will it do? What problems is it going to solve? Will it make a part of life better? Which bit?

These are all questions that you need to answer in order to move forward with your idea. Perhaps the most important part is determining what problem your app is going to solve. This is a basic rule of business – the idea is that your app has to help a target market to do something that is going to make their lives easier.

If you haven't yet thought of an idea for your app now is a good time to do that. So, take a pen and paper and start brainstorming. What are the problems you want to solve? Think about your own life first, and what parts of it could be solved with an app. It doesn't matter if it's a huge problem or a tiny little one; make a list of every single problem you can think of. If you can't think of anything, make sure you have a pen and pepper with you at all times and, as you go through the course of a normal day, be more observant. Note down any problems that come screaming out at you. Not just yours either – think about the people around you. Ask them if there is anything they think an app could help them with. Listen to conversations going on around you and concentrate on "problem keywords":

- "I hate..."

- "This sucks/isn't right/could be better"

- "I wish..."

Keep your ears open, you might be surprised at just how often you hear these words or others like them. A simple word with the people saying them will soon have your paper full of ideas that you could potentially solve with an app.

Start Drawing

By drawing out the ideas for the app, you are, in effect, laying down the foundation for the interface that will form part of your app. You need to visualize the features in your app, the layout and the structure. These are just approximations at this stage, something that you can work with later on down the line.

Some of the most important developers in the world place most of the importance of an app on the design. It is, without a doubt, the most crucial part. Have a wander through the app stores and look at the sheer numbers of apps. Do you ever wonder why lots of them fail? I'll tell you – design. Think about this scenario:

There are two apps, both priced the same, both have the same function and the same extra features. To all intents and purposes, they could be clones of one another. Except of on thing – one of the apps has a design look that is inconsistent and messy while the other flows well, is sleek, clean and easy to use. Which one are you going to choose? The same as everyone else – the good-looking one. It doesn't even matter if the features aren't up to standard of the former app; because it looks good, people will buy it.

When we talk about design though, we are not just talking about how it looks but also how it feels. You need to remember that the interface you are designing is what people use to interact with your app. You might have some fantastic features in it but if people can't use them properly then it's all been a waste of time.

You also need to keep in mind that each different platform has their own methods and presentations but the principles of design remain pretty much the same – they must have usability. If your audience can't use or play your app, it will fail; it's as simple as that. You don't actually get to decide if your app has usability or not – the consumers get that job and it's what they think that you have to worry about.

One way to make your apps more usable is though a good interface design. Use colors intelligently to make different parts stand out; add in intuitive controls; don't put too much on each screen; don't go overboard with fancy fonts and colors. These are just some of the things you have to think about to make your app more usable.

iOS Apps

When it comes to designing an iOS app, Apple provides lots of different custom templates. However, these are only for apps that are not games. Apple provides all of the tools you need to get your idea into reality with the right design, quickly and easily. However, while it may be convenient to use a template, you should try to code from scratch, its good practice. Again, Apple provides a style guide for you to get some idea from and it can give you a lot of good ideas. Not only that, if you conform to the style guide, you will significantly raise your chances of the app passing Apple's strict checking procedures for acceptance into the app store.

Android

On the Android developer's website, there is a page that gives you all the information you need to know about designing your app. It tells you what elements you need to include, and goes over the principles of designing an app. The page has been produced by the Android developer community, people who are doing this all day, very day and, when you are stuck on something, there really isn't a better place to go for the answers.

As well as that, there is also an Android design ask that you can download, containing all the materials you need to get started on your design. That includes color swatches, stencils, icon packs and much more besides. This will save you a great deal of time and effort and will speed up the entire proves.

Windows

Windows Mobile is relatively new so you won't find so much in the way of templates to use. However, on the Windows developer site, you will find a design guide that tells you all you need to know and gives lots of pointers to put you in the right direction.

Research

Research is vital for developing an app, and you need to research the following four areas:

Are there any other apps that do the same as yours?

Look for inspiration for the design of your app

Look for information on the technical requirements of your app

Find information on how to market your app and monetize it.

You might think that your idea is unique but you could find your hopes dashed in an instant. There are almost 2 million Android and iOS apps out there, not including the other platforms so it is going to be next to impossible to come up with a unique app. However, don't let this stop you. You must focus your attention on your project and not all the other apps. Use those apps to give you ideas (but do not copy) and learn from their mistakes and the key features they put in them.

The technical aspects of your app are important. You need to find out exactly what they are and what you need to take into account when you are building the app. This will also give you some idea of whether your app will actually work or not form a technical viewpoint. You might find that it doesn't but you will also find options for continuing but along a slightly different route. Include research on privacy and copyright.

Marketing and monetization ae the last two bits of research you need to do at this stage. Once you know your app can be built you, need to start thinking about how you are going to market it. It's no good building an app if no one knows about it so, think about your niche and find out the best ways to target your audience; how to approach them and how to get the value of your app across. Then think about how your app is going to make money. Are you going to charge for the app? Will you give it away free but have ads on it? There are lots of ways you can make money off an app so give this considerable thought.

Wireframe and Storyboard

Now it's time for your ideas to start coming together with the features you want to add in. Wireframing is a great way of bringing your ideas together into something that is easier to see. In short, a wireframe is a skeleton of the app, similar on a small scale to the blueprints of a building. It is the backbone of the app and it lays out the hierarchy, structure and the relationships between the elements that go into your app.

The idea is to focus on what the screen is doing and not what its looks like. You are not supposed to add in color or graphics to a wireframe, or any other styles and they are certainly not the end design. The process of designing a mobile app is a long one and wireframes are a great help in keeping you on track each step of the way, and help you to refine things later on.

How Long Does a Wireframe Last?

Wireframes must begin at a very early part of the process of designing your app but it must also continue throughout the process. It is a powerful and ongoing part that allows you to see your app building up bit by bit. It allows you to work out where everything fits together and, although it sounds like a long drawn out task, it actually isn't. Before you try to create the first look and feel of your app, you should create a wireframe for each section. Every possibly way of interacting and every possible result must be planned our and designed so that your app works, no matter how it is used. The wireframe will last until your app is built.

Are wireframes meant to show layout only?

Yes, in a word. A wireframe shows you whether your app will be usable by letting you see and move through each section. It guides you through a complete visualization of the app without the distraction of graphics and design that can draw your attention away from the core of the app. The more you are engaged in wireframing, the more ideas and concepts you will have, and the end result will be an intuitive app that is fully functional and user-friendly.

While you are at it, create a storyboard, a visual map that shows the connection between the screens and shows how the user can move through the app, laying out all possible scenarios.

Define the Back End of Your App

With your wireframes and your storyboard, you can now begin the task of building the back end of your app. Draw up a sketch of the servers, data diagrams and APIs. This is a good reference point for when you come to develop the app and also gives you an ongoing diagram that is self-explanatory for reference. If there are any evident technical limitations, modify your storyboard and wireframes accordingly.

Test out Your Prototype

Ask other people to take a look at your storyboard and wireframes, tell you what they think of it. Ask them to give the app a test and then ask them to provide honest feedback. You need to know if there are any flaws or dead ends that need to be fixed. Ask them to try out the prototype while you are there so that you can see how they use it; watch their actions and then modify your interface accordingly.

The goal here is to get as much done and done right before you move onto the full design process. Once you begin that, it will be a lot harder to shift things around so make it as clear as possible right from the start.

Build the Back End

Now that you have defined your app, it's time to start building the back end. You will need to have several things set up – servers, APIs, databases and storage. One other thing you must do at this stage is sign up for a developer account with the platform you are designing for. It may take a few days for your account to be approved so don't leave it until the last minute.

Design the Skins

Skins are the separate screens that you need for the app. Your job at this stage is to create the high-resolution versions of your wireframes. Now you must take into account all of the comments your prototype testers make because, after all, the idea is to build an app that your audience will use. Feedback from testers should help you to provide the perfect user interface.

Test it Again

Once the skins are complete, you need to test it again. What you've done so far may look pretty good but there is a long way to go. At this stage, your app concept will be in place for your testers to see, with all the graphics and the text, as you want it to be. Now you can test your app to see how it really feels and looks.

There are a couple of ways to test your app at this stage, using app testing software or people. Find a suitable one and import your designs in, with the right links so that the flow from screen to screen can be fully tested out. You can also use human testers as well.

Do not confuse this stage with the wireframing stage. That was about the framework for how the app would look and feel; this is all about the actual design and how it all works together

Revise and Keep Building

As soon as you have test driven your app and got more feedback, you can take on board the comments from the testers and use them to give your app more polishing. At this stage, there is still time to change the layout and thee is still time to make changes on the back end.

Refine it

As you go through the build process, you should be constantly looking at your app as each stage is developed. With Android, it is very easy to install the app on a mobile device to test it out in a live environment. iOS isn't as easy as that – you will need to download a specific test platform that you download your app onto and test it out through each stage. This is the final step in the development process and you can use this to constantly monitor your app until it is complete and is ready for release.

Time for Release

When it comes to accepting apps into their stores, each platform has its own set of policies. Android will let your app straight into the app store without reviewing it, although they will get to it at some stage. Once again, iOS is different. Apple will not allow an app into their store until it has been tested and approved. They don't set a timescale but expect it to be at least 7 days, most likely more, before you hear back from them with an answer.

You can submit your newly built app to a serve called PreApps. This allows you to reach out to those who like to be first to try out a new app and you can get some very early feedback on your brand new masterpiece.

So, those are the steps that you need to follow to be successful at building your app. I have not gone into details about how to write and code your app because that is a subject for another book and relies entirely upon the platform that you choose to use.

Chapter 4: Sample Android App Development

It's time to get your hand on simple app development. This section will give you a run down of the procedures involved in creating your first Android app project.

Prepare the Environment

The environment refers to the app development platform to be used. It will process codes and generate preview of the outcome. The first step is to download Android Studio and the latest SDK tools via SDK Manager.

Android Studio is the app development platform offered by Android developers. It runs using intelligent code editor capable of analyzing codes, refactoring and other advance coding techniques.

Before downloading Android Studio, be sure the platform is compatible with your system. Minimum system requirements are the following for three main operating systems.

System Components	Windows	Mac	Linux
Operating System	Vista/7/8, 32 or 64-bit	OS X 10.8.5 or later, up to 10.9	GNOME or KDE Desktop
Hard Disk Space	400 MB	400 MB	400 MB
Minimum RAM (Recommended RAM)	2 GB (4 GB)	2 GB (4 GB)	2 GB (4 GB)
Minimum Space for Android SDK and emulators	1 GB	1 GB	1 GB
Minimum Screen Resolution	1280 x 800	1280 x 800	1280 x 800
Development Kits	Java Development Kit (JD) 7	Java Development Kit (JD) 7	Java Development Kit (JD) 7
Other Platforms		Java Runtime Environ	GNU C Library (glibc) 2.15

		ment (JRE) 6	or higher

The SDK Manager is a system that separates SDK tools, platforms and other vital programming solutions into packages. It's advisable to get the latest SDK tools, which shouldn't be a problem as the SDK Manager installs the latest tool versions by default. The manager is installed together with Android Studio and can be launched by going to Tools menu then look for Android. The SDK Manager should be available under the Android tool set.

Start creating your app project after installing Android Studio.

Creating an App Interface

Launch Android Studio and you will be greeted with a Welcome screen. Look for *New Project* and it will direct you to the next dialog box where you can configure project details. It will ask you for four main details—the App Name, Company Domain, Package name, and Project location. App Name is basically the name you want to give an app. Details doesn't have to be formal.

Company domain is your company's website or domain name. This will append to new app developed, which will be helpful for app marketing. For now, you can type any domain for practice. Edit this field later once you're ready to build an app for sale.

Filling out the company domain will also fill out the *package name*. Edit this part later by clicking the *Edit* link.

Project location is the folder where the app project files will be stored. Complete all these details and hit Next.

The next page will limit the minimum Android OS version where the app will run. For *Minimum SDK*, choose *API 8: Android 2.2 (Froyo)*. This means that Froyo is the earliest app version compatible with your app. You can choose other preferred minimum SDK option. Leave all the entries without changing then hit *Next*.

Look for *Add an activity to <template>*. Choose *Blank Activity* then hit *Next*. Activity refers to the unique Android feature that allows access to the program. A basic and main activity for user is launching the app. However, developers can further enhance the app by adding other activities.

After setting the activity, configure other options needed for running the app. Look for *Choose options for your new file*. Under this option, configure *Activity Name* and edit it to *MyActivity*. Change Layout name and Title to activity_my and MyActivity, respectively. The Menu Resource Name will have menu_my as its value. Hit Finish to complete the project. Completing this project results to a simple "Hello World" app that come complete with basic default files.

Several vital codes must be kept in mind as fundamental codes that introduce you to app development. See the following codes and their functions.

app/src/main/res/layout/activity_my.xml

This XML code represents the activity you set with your project. It generates a simple user interface preview with text view showing the text "Hello World!"

app/build.gradle

Gradle is a file used for compiling and building the mobile app project. Each project module comes with its own *build.gradle* file, as well as a universal build.gradle file for the completed project. A developer usually concentrates on app module *build.gradle* file. Other dependencies are configured together with build.gradle file like *compiledSdkVersion*, *minSdkVersion*, *targetSdkversion*, and a lot more, which you'll learn in advanced app programming.

app/src/main/java/com.mycompany.myfirstapp/MyActivity.java

Take note that some details on the code are the ones filled out at the beginning of app development. This code is responsible for running the Activity class code, which will load its corresponding activity and show the layout file containing "Hello World!"

Running the App

Now that your simple app is ready to go, it's time to test it out by running it on multiple platforms. You can run the app through the actual device or through an emulator. Running the app on both platforms require Android Studio for installation and loading. Command line can also be used to load the newly developed app.

Testing on Actual Portable Device Using Android Studio

In testing the app on a real device, you need to install the app first using a different method than the traditional way of installing apps from Google Play. Set up the device plugging it in your development machine (or computer) using its USB cable. You may need to install necessary drivers to detect the device. Refer to your device's manual to follow driver installation procedures if it's your first time to do so.

Once plugged in, activate USB debugging feature on the portable device. This feature can be found in different locations depending on the device's OS version. Devices with earlier Android OS up to Android 3.2 has this option under Settings> Applications> Development. Newer devices starting from Android 4.0 has the option under Settings> Development options.

Load Android Studio then look for your project's file. Hit *Run*, a command found on the toolbar area. It will let you choose a device for operating the app. From *Choose Device*, tick *Choose a running device* option, then *OK*. It will then install the app then load accordingly.

Test on Portable Device Using Command Line

Running the app via command line requires manual coding. Open the usual command line and look for project directory files, which was set right at the beginning of app development. Using Gradle file, this procedure will create the app's .apk file, or the file similar to compressed file that can be transferred to portable devices and installed manually.

After navigating to the project folder, type *gradlew.bat assembleDebug for Windows platforms* or *$ chmod +x gradlew and $ ./gradlew assembleDebug* for Mac and Linux systems. Take note that the commands for Mac and Linux should be separated into two lines, with both line starting with the dollar sign. Doing this command will then build the .apk file.

From there, you should begin running the app on the command line with the command *adb install app/build/outputs/MyFirstApp-debug.apk*. It will install the app on the device, which you will search for manually. The app is named *MyFirstApp*. Open it and it should run on your device.

Testing on Emulator with Android Studio

Aside from running the sample app on the actual device, it's also possible to run the app using an emulator. An emulator is a platform that mimics your target device's environment. It has settings similar to the target device, giving you a complete picture of how the app should look like once it's loaded on the actual device.

Just like in running the app on an actual device, you will also need Android Studio or command line to operate the app on top of an actual emulator.

Create an Android Virtual Device (AVD) by going to *Android Studio>Tools >Android >AVD Manager.* Look for AVD Manager icon to list all available emulator environment. Details found on the emulator includes Phone models, profiles, screen resolution, and target Android OS. Don't be surprised to see phone models listed on the emulator. When one of these profiles are selected, the emulator will load the same environment that the specific model has for accurate app testing.

On the AVD Manager, look for *Create Virtual Device* then select for preferred device configuration. Click *Next*. Select system version to load then load Next. Check configuration settings and verify. Hit *Finish* to complete setup.

Follow the same procedures for running Android Studio. But instead of selecting *Choose a running device*, choose *Launch Emulator.* Click the Android virtual device and click the drop-down menu to look for preferred emulator configuration. Click *OK*.

Wait for the emulator to load. Once loaded, it may ask you to unlock the screen like in an actual device. Unlock and wait for the app to load on the screen.

Testing App on Emulator Using Command Line

Follow the same procedures for coding and running app on actual device to build its .apk file. Open emulator and look for MyFirstApp. Open and wait for the app to load.

This app is quite simple, but it's a good start in knowing the fundamentals of app development. In time, you can use Android Studio to create a better looking user interface for your app.

Chapter 5: Sample iOS App Development

The number of Apple device users also posed a demand for newer and better iOS apps. Just like Android app development, iOS app development becomes easier with Swift programming language and Xcode, the brand's own integrated development environment (IDE).

One of the sample app development guide provided by Apple developers is a food-tracking app that allows multiple activities like adding or removing meals on the list. The entire app development begins with downloading all needed resources and tools.

Prepare the Environment

Xcode is the platform complete with all features needed for designing, creating and debugging developed apps. The platform also comes with iOS

SDK tools ranging from compilers, frameworks and other tools that guarantee stable app development.

Run the Mac App Store installed with the operating system, usually found in the Dock. Type *Xcode* in the search field then hit the Return key. The platform should appear as the first search result. Click the result then install the platform by following its included instruction. The following page will ask you for Apple ID. Type your ID and password to complete the download. The downloaded file should be found in the */Applications* directory.

Aside from Xcode, users will also benefit from downloading Swift playground. Playground is a type of file that allows codes to interact with the changes you made and be able to see the outcome immediately. Seeing the outcome straightaway speeds up the learning curve in understanding essential Swift concepts. Apple threw in a sample playground on its website for developers to use with Xcode for testing.

Being an introduction to app development, Swift essential codes won't be discussed in detail in this book. But to give you an idea, the following are some concepts encountered on the actual coding process.

- **Constant.** Constant refers to unchangeable value after declaration. Use the syntax *let* to declare a constant.

- **Variable.** Variable is a changeable value in a code and declared using *var*.

- **String interpolation.** This process is the easier way of including values needed in a string. It's coded using backslash before the parenthesis indicating the string.

- **Optionals.** An optional refers to a possibly missing value in a code. A value is marked as an option by placing a question mark after the syntax.

- **Array.** An array refers to the data type that tracks a collection of items according to their order. Arrays are marked using brackets.

- **Conditional statements.** A conditional statement is a type of control flow statement using syntaxes like *if* and *switch*. This statement checks the statement first to see if the declared condition is true before executing the code.

- **Loops.** A loop is another control flow statement that repeats code execution multiple times. Its syntaxes include *while* and *for-in*.

- **If statement.** An if statement will check and verify if a declared condition is true. If the condition is true, the statement will generate the outcome according to the code.

- **Else.** An else statement is a clause added to if statement that promotes more complex control flow. Else indicates what the code should do next if the conditional statement turns out to be false.

- **Switch.** A switch statement works with all data types and supports numerous comparison operations. It switches the value of a declared string.

- **Function.** A function refers to a small code that can be used multiple times in a program. It's coded using *func* syntax.

- **Class.** A class refers to a blueprint-like component for an object that provides additional information about their properties.

- **Object.** An object refers to a class instance declared in a code.

- **Enumerations.** Enumerations describe or declare a common type for clusters with related values. Coded as *enum*.

- **Structures.** A structure is a component that supports an array of classes, initializers and other vital code components. Coded as *struct*.

- **Protocol.** A protocol describes a blueprint or framework of properties, methods and functions supporting a specific functionality or feature. Represented by *protocol* syntax.

- **Cocoa Touch.** Cocoa Touch is a collection of Apple frameworks utilized with iOS app development.

Developing a Basic User Interface

Creating a simple user interface for the food-tracking app sample is easy with Xcode. Aside from learning codes the easy way, users will also see the outcome with the Simulator, another platform that gives users a preview of how the app will look like on actual devices.

Begin by creating the project. Launch Xcode from its download directory. The program will load the welcome screen. Choose *Create a new Xcode project* then choose *Application* where you can choose your template. As a beginner, select *Single View Application*. This view means the app will have a single-page interface, the simplest layout option in the platform. Hit *Next* after choosing the layout.

The next dialog box is similar to Android Studio where you'll fill out project details. Details asked are the following:

- **Product Name.** Fill out this field with your preferred app name.

- **Organization Name.** This refers to your company or organization name. You can leave this blank.

- **Language.** This means the type of language used for programming, which *Swift*.

- **Bundle Identifier.** This field's value will automatically generate after typing the app name, organization name, and organization identifier.

- **Devices.** This lets you configure the app's compatibility with different Apple devices. Choose *Universal*, which means the app will run on both iPad and iPhone.

- **Organization Identifier.** This is where the organization identifier will go for people with such data. If a user doesn't have an organization identifier, simply use com.example as a dummy identifier.

Additional configuration settings are also found on the same dialog box. They focus on testing user interfaces and other data. Settings should be the following:

- **Include UI Tests.** Don't tick this option.

- **Include Unit Tests.** Check to select.

- **Use Core Data.** Don't tick the check box.

Once every data is field, hit *Next* to be directed to the next window. This next page will ask you to choose a storage location for project files. Select preferred folder or location then click Create. Doing this will direct you to the workspace windows.

The workspace is divided into four parts or areas:

- **Toolbar.** The top most part is composed of toolbars to use for generating the user interface.

- **Editor Area.** This is the middle part of the platform that takes the most space. It's meant for configuring or editing app layouts and essential interface sections.

- **Navigator Area.** It's the panel found on the left side of the program that lists project folders, storyboard files, and other data compiled for the project.

- **Utility Area.** Located at the right part of the screen, this panel has data and utilities required for setting the project up.

Preview the App via Simulator

The advantage of using a layout and configuring the app's details is you already have the basic app ready. However, it looks bare by having a simple white background and plain text for the app name. You can view this bare app by running the simulator.

Look for the *Scheme* popup menu at the Toolbar area. Select preferred device like *iPhone 6*. It will let you choose to run a Simulator or device where you want to test the app. Choose *iPhone 6 Simulator* and not the actual iPhone 6 device. Look for the *Run* icon that looks like a play icon on music players at the top left corner of the toolbar.

If it's your first time to run an app on Xcode, it will ask if you prefer to enable the debugging features for the platform. Choose which option you prefer then follow the succeeding prompts.

Wait for the toolbar to complete the project. The platform is done building the app once it loaded the simulator and the preview of your app. It will show the splash screen with the app name then another blank page, which is probably for the succeeding pages to create.

Take note that the simulator's screen size will change depending on the device type. In choosing an iPhone device simulator, you will see the screen as the usual rectangular smartphone display. For iPads, you'll see a wider display with different orientation than those of smartphones.

Once you're done viewing the app, close the simulator by going to Simulator menu and selecting *Quit Simulator*. Pressing *Command+Q* will also close the simulator, but faster without navigating through Xcode.

Other procedures will be required to create a good app interface that will sell in stores. You will learn more about designing iOS apps in detail upon trying out guides for advanced users. In the meantime, download playgrounds and codes of sample app development then use them with Xcode for practice.

Chapter 6: Sample Windows App Development

In the past, Android and iOS emerged as the two main mobile device operating systems competing for consumers and developers' attention. However, Windows phones entered the picture and began sharing their app features for portable device users. As the new kid on the block, it doesn't have as much apps to offer to device users, which can be a good market for developers once Windows phones began to pick up in the market.

Developing Windows apps also require specific platforms like Visual Studio, the developers program and app development tool. Windows also support multiple programming languages to suit developers' preference. Programming language options include C# and XAML, JavaScript with HTML, and C++ with XAML.

Windows makes development easier for beginners by setting up a designated development website where all needed resources, development tools, and sample codes are available for download.

In developing newer universal Windows mobile apps, developers recommend getting Windows 10, its latest operating system online. Take note of minimum system requirement in running this operating system.

Prepare the Environment

Set up the app development environment by downloading the latest version of Visual Studio 2015. Those who have Visual Studio can update their current copy to use for development. Developers can also go online to download the Microsoft Visual Studio Community 2015, a free platform that includes simulators for testing the app.

Download the Visual Studio Community 2015 and custom install programs including the *Universal Windows App Development Tools*. Under this option are *Tools and Windows SDK 10.0.10240* and *Emulators for Windows Mobile 10.0.10240*. Check all three features then hit *Next* to install.

Aside from development platforms, all Windows devices and desktops must be enabled to support app development. Apps will fail to deploy if all devices are not activated to support app development. Each device and desktop has different ways of development activation.

For Windows 10 desktop, phones and tablets, choose *Settings> Update & Security> For developers*. This will give you three settings that will let you install and test apps. Your main options are *Sideload apps* and *Developer mode*.

Developer mode allows you to debug installed apps on the devices. It can also sideload apps. Choosing this option is making your devices a testing tool for your apps. However, don't install other apps that you don't trust in this mode as it may cause inconsistencies and stop your device from running accordingly.

Sideload apps option is an option that allows installation of trusted app. However, it will require certificate to install apps. The device should have these certificates and approved to run the device without worries. If your current app's certificate is in the device, you can install the project app.

For Windows 10 desktops, users can enable this feature through the registry for Windows 10 Home Edition or *gpedit.msc* for other operating system versions.

For Windows 10 Home Edition, open command prompt and run as administrator to apply changes in the computer. Run *regedit* and wait for the registry to load. Look for the following folders and change DWORD values to *1*, which means enabling or activating support for specific function:

HKLM\SOFTWARE\Microsoft\Windows\Curre ntVersion\AppModelUnlock\AllowAllTrustedA pps

HKLM\SOFTWARE\Microsoft\Windows\Curre ntVersion\AppModelUnlock\AllowDevelopmen tWithoutDevLicense

These two registry entries are the same with Sideload apps and Developer mode in portable devices.

For other Windows 10 versions, run *gpedit.msc*. Look for *Local Computer Policy*. Look for *Computer Configuration> Administrative Templates> Windows Components> App Package Deployment*. Configure the policies and enable the options *Allow all trusted apps to install* (for sideloading apps) and *Allows development of Windows Store apps and installing them from an integrated development environment (IDE)* (for Developer mode).

Setting these all up means your devices are ready for development.

Registering as a Developer

Several guides include developer's registration as one of the first things to do in app development. Registration is not necessary if you're still learning app development. This is only for those who plan to sell their apps that are ready for publishing. Wait until you master app development before registering as a developer.

Create a Basic App

Even in loading Visual Studio, you still need to select your preferred programming language. This guide will use C# as the main programming language. Navigate your way from *Installed> Templates> Visual C#> Windows> Universal* from the left panel. Look at the right side of the program and see the list of templates available. Choose *Blank App (Universal Windows)*. The *Solution Explorer* will show you one project, which is the default option because the template itself is adaptive. Developers can add other pages if preferred and further enhance them according to desired features.

Preview App

Although your current app is still bare, you can preview it using the designer feature that supports device configuration of your choice. Look for the drop down menu above the designer or editor area. Click the drop down button and see a list of devices with their sizes, screen resolution, and other option for preview. Select preferred device and orientation to see how your app will look like.

Running the App

Testing your app can be done by running it using a simulator or testing it on an actual device. Test your device locally or using a simulator by going to *Standard* toolbar and look for *Local Machine* button. The same button has a drop down arrow for choosing your preferred testing platform. Options include *Simulator*, *Local Machine*, *Device*, *Remote Machine*, and other mobile emulator choices. Select local machine or simulator to run the app on your current system.

If you prefer to see the app on an actual Windows device, select an emulator or attach the portable device to your computer.

Chapter 7: Introduction to High-End App Development

The last three chapters taught you about building a simple app interface using various platforms and previewing them in simulators or emulators. In time, you'll be well-versed in app development and find coding way easier.

Expert developers came up with a lot of integrated features with their high-end applications. Although you won't learn the techniques for now, it's good to know these integrated features to give you an idea in developing your future app.

Integrated Multimedia

These apps are among the most fun apps to use with their multimedia-rich development. They allow people to watch videos, listen to music, or even take pictures then share them with friends. Developing these apps require proper communication between the app itself and multimedia content to run flawlessly.

Integrated Content Sharing System

Most users today find the importance of content sharing through their mobile phones and tablets. They can access files wherever they go and continue collaborating with their colleagues even without access to their computers. Through content sharing, users will have access to files, comment on uploaded contents, see access history, and others.

Integrated Cloud and Connectivity

Apps today generally need internet connection to access content or media stored online. Integrating internet connectivity features to mobile apps is complicated and would require knowledge of both app development and network behavior.

Aside from internet connectivity, some high-end apps support cloud storage access. Cloud storage allows people to gain access to their files without using desktop computers and download them directly to their devices. Developing these apps require knowledge of file syncing to ensure proper function.

Integrated Animation and Graphics

Majority of mobile device users prefer graphics-rich apps with animations that make app use more enjoyable than before. Apps with animations and graphics require precise resource allotment to ensure seamless performance and boost their edge when marketed in app stores.

Integrated User Info

Apps like mobile banking and email apps require user authentication by typing their credentials. These apps must be developed accordingly for secure account access and avoid giving access to people who placed wrong credentials.

Aside from accessing a single platform, integrated user information also allows apps to identify user details to access all other accounts like in the case of Google accounts. A person needs one account to access Google Plus, Gmail, Google Play, Docs and other Google services. Communication in between these platforms is possible with their superb coding architecture.

Integrated Maps

Countless apps today are developed to help people with directions or simply monitoring their current locations. Mapping information allows users to know their locations accurately with the help of other features that boost their function like GPS. Integrating GPS with map-enabled apps is a complex process and would require a lot of training before completing a single project.

Chapter 8: Best Practices for Developing an Impeccable App

Technical knowledge in building an app is one thing. However, some best practices can help you create the perfect app that users can't wait to purchase, regardless of your chosen mobile OS.

Create a User Interface that Suits All Devices

Technological development resulted to different mobile devices with varying features. Your goal as a developer is to create an app with user interface compatible with all devices possible. An app with impeccable design won't be as marketable if people can't load them properly on their devices.

Focus on Performance

Performance is king in developing apps. For mobile device users, an app that crash intermittently is junk and will be uninstalled right away. They will even leave negative feedback on your developer's profile to warn people in downloading your app.

With proper planning, coding and the right tools, you can create a highly responsive app that will run without crashing unless the device itself experienced inconsistency.

Consider Battery Life

Running an app also consumes energy. With people's lifestyle today, they access a lot of mobile apps, browse websites, watch videos, stream music, and other activities through their mobile phones. All these activities consume a lot of battery, so many mobile device users prefer apps that use as little battery as possible.

What many novice developers don't know is that energy efficiency is possible in app development. With proper training and the right tool, developers can produce a responsive app that doesn't drain battery.

Don't Forget App and Data Security

App security is crucial for many people, especially for those accessing financial accounts through mobile apps. If you're thinking of developing an app that requires user's info for access, don't forget to improve your app's security features, ensuring every data is encrypted to prevent unauthorized access.

Think About User Input Choices

Typing data on user info pages or search engines is the usual user input option across all devices. However, many users prefer other options like touch screen gestures that allow them to access apps. Proper development gives way to efficient and accurate communication between the input choice and the app.

Aside from the device's on-display keyboards, some users prefer using external hardware keyboards connected through wireless connection. Combining seamless communication between the app, hardware and connectivity device ensures users will use their preferred input choice.

Test Apps Accordingly

Testing apps before publishing is like a standard procedure for developers. There are different ways of testing apps. You will learn a lot of testing procedures for Android, iOS, and Windows apps to ensure they are ready to impress once published.

Background Jobs Must be Minimized

Other activities run together with the app. These are called background jobs or activities. While they are important app components to bridge functions, they consume a lot of power and affect apps' performance. They also trigger app crashes.

App development guides will help you create an app with minimized background jobs to save battery and ensure high quality performance at all times.

Create an Interactive and Engaging App

Your goals in developing an app is to encourage people to download and continue app usage. Let users gain access to content as fast as possible to keep them from being bored with your app. Integrate other visual components that will keep people from recommending your app and updating their current app versions.

Conclusion

I would like to thank you for downloading my books and I hope it was helpful to you. I have tried to give you some guidance on how to get into and be successful in the mobile app development world. Mobile apps do take time and effort to design, develop and build but they can be rewarding in a financial sense as well as a sense of achievement.

The ideas in this book require you to go away and do some research, learn a bit about programming and get to grips with the platform you have chosen. Once you start learning, don't stop. Experience is invaluable and things change on an almost daily basis with app development so you need to keep on top of things.

Once again, thanks for downloading my book; if you found it helpful, please leave a review for me at Amazon.com

Free Bonus ($9.99): Get My Latest Kindle E-Book "Top 10 Gadgets of 2015" for Free

As a "Thank You" for purchasing, and reading my book I would like to send you my latest E-book "Top 10 Gadgets of 2015" for F.R.E.E. This is no strings attached offer, just my gift to you for being a great customer. Just Click on the image below

https://cracklifecode.leadpages.net/technology/